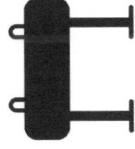
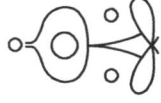

Child's Play

A rhyming active, interactive book

www.annastylesauthor.com

Anna Styles 2019
St Helier, Jersey

Text copyright: Anna Styles 2019
Illustrations: Canva

1 2 3 4 5 6 7 8 9 10

ISBN (Paperback):978-1-9162343-3-8
ISBN (e-book): 978-1-9162343-2-1

Don't just read.
Imagine, pretend, play!

For my sporty husband James and my son Luca, who is eagerly following in his footsteps xx

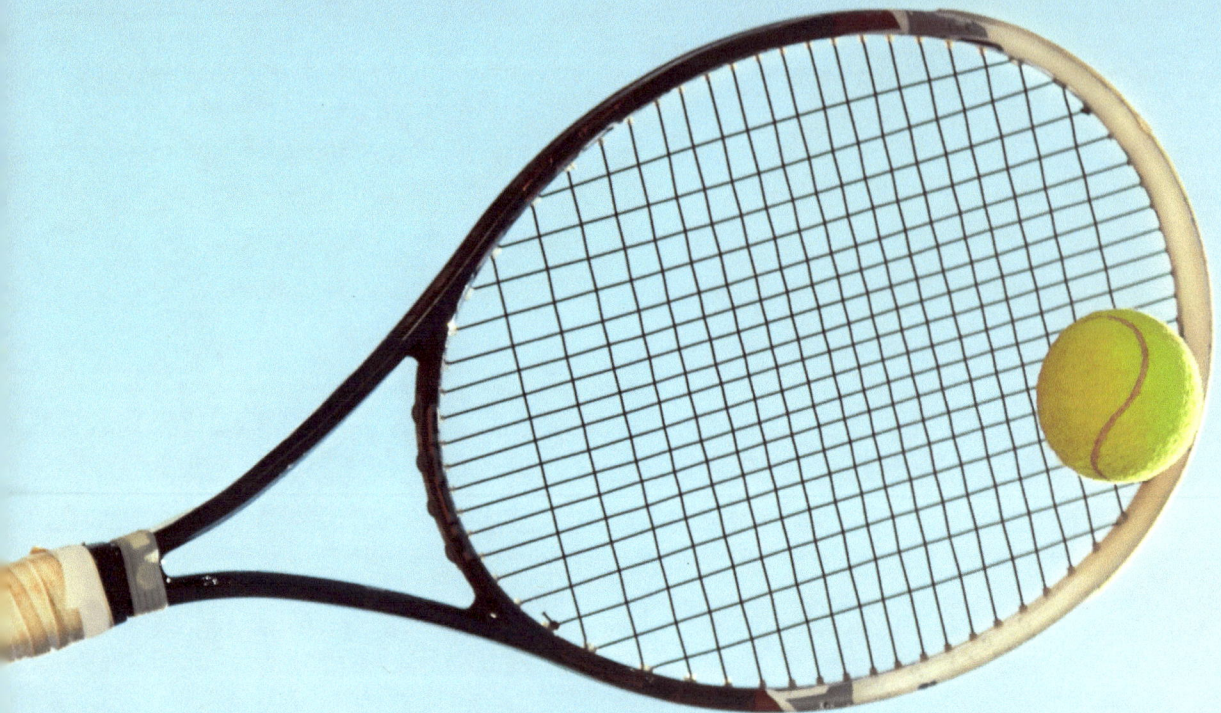

Tennis

Pick up your racquet, stand in the right place,
Throw the ball in the air and serve an ace,

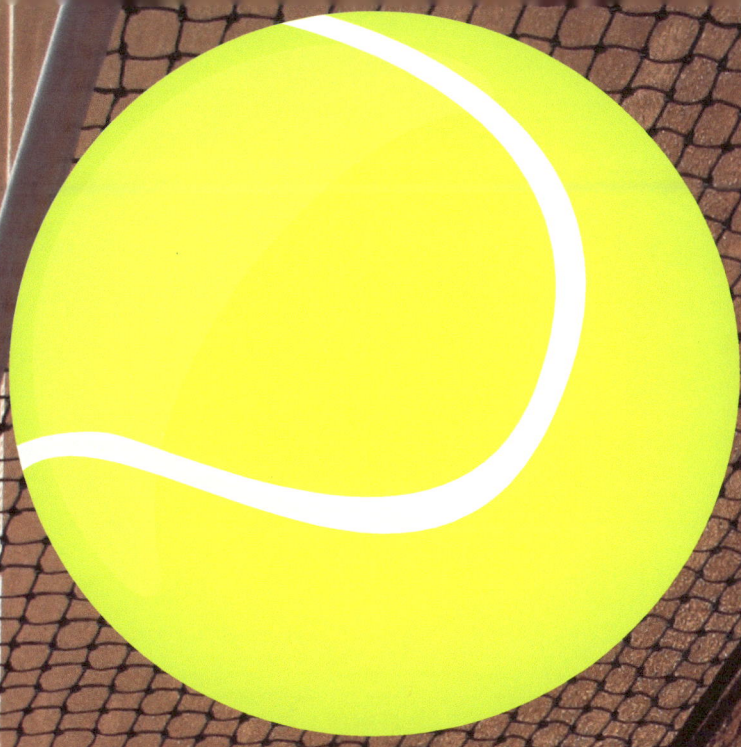

Then lob a volley over the net,
Run for the point and work up a sweat.

AT THE *pool*

Swimming

Now it's time to dive into the pool,
Lie on your tummy and do front crawl.

So circle your arms and kick your feet,
If you swim fast you might win your heat.

Trampolining

Jump up high on the big trampoline.

That's the best jump I've ever seen!

Try a tummy tuck, then a star jump.

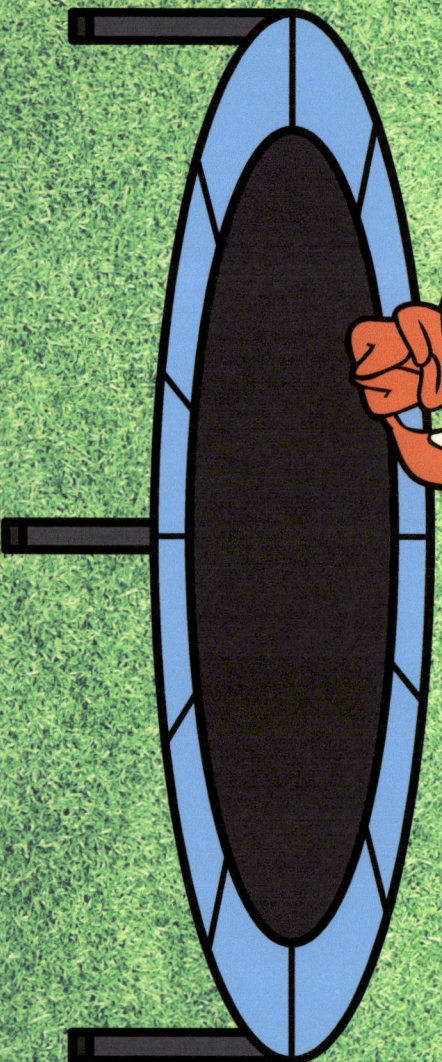

Wow!

That was great, you deserve a fist pump.

Football

Dribble around me here on the floor.
With the next kick, it's time to score.

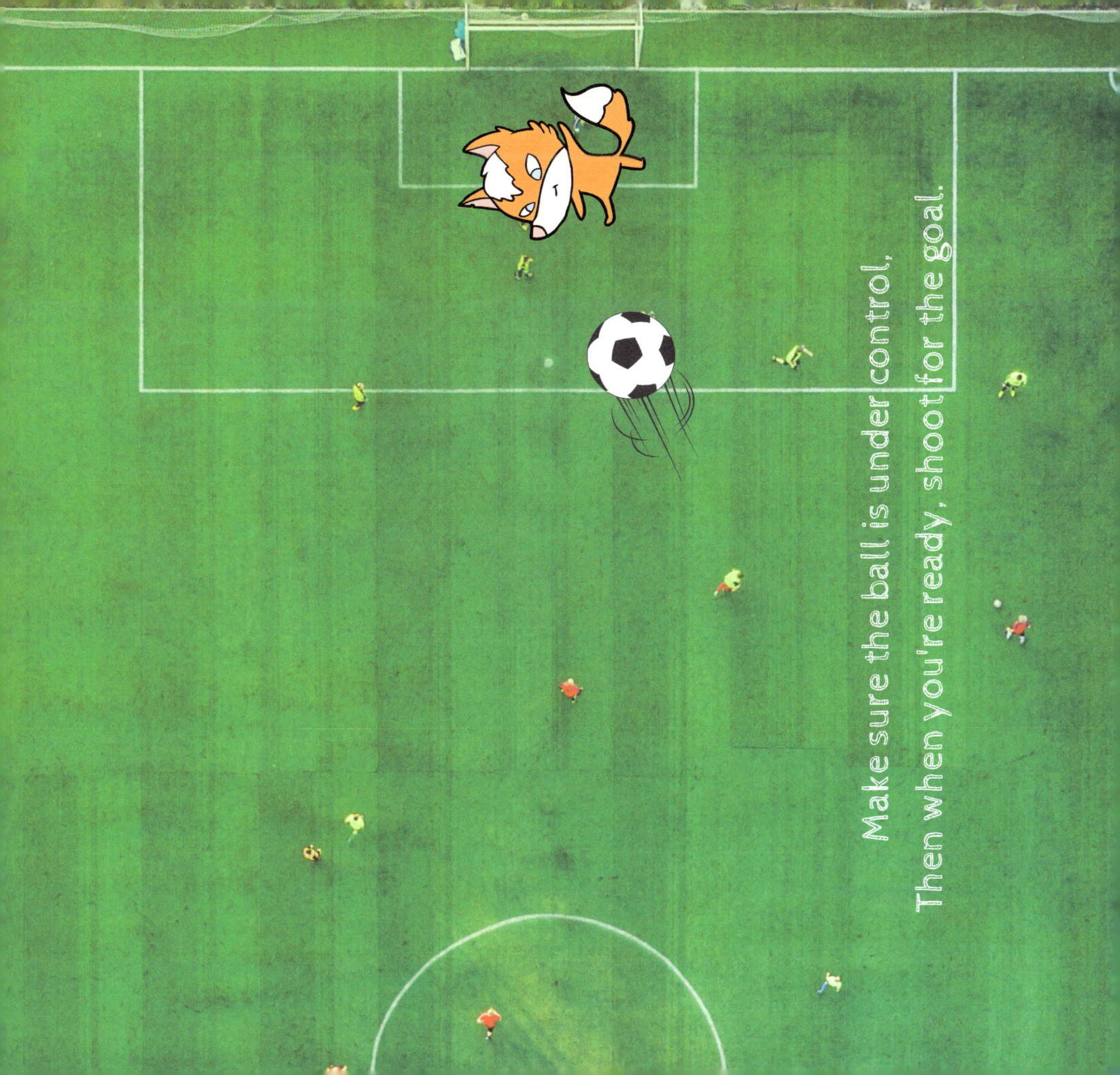

Make sure the ball is under control.

Then when you're ready, shoot for the goal.

Running

Time to run, tie your laces up tight.

First, we warm up, stretch up to full height.

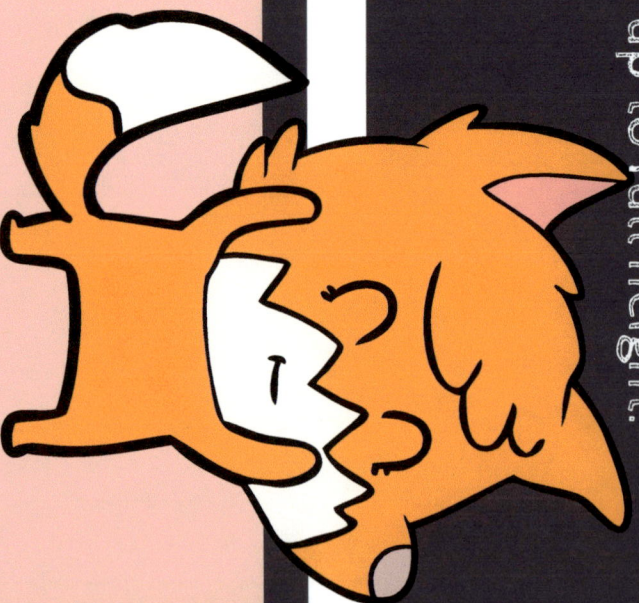

Run as fast as you can to beat your best time.

Ready? Set. Go!
Cross the finish line.

Before you swing, put your ball on the tee.
Now hit it hard, avoiding the tree.

Golf

Time to putt the ball into the hole.

Tap it gently, aim for the pole.

Dancing

Arms in the air, let go and have fun.
It's time to dance, the music's begun.

Imagine you're wearing your best outfit.

And throw some shapes to the latest hit.

Lie on your back, put your legs in the air.
Circle them round, as fast as you dare.
You're cycling fast down a mountain track.

Cycling

Now uphill, is it hard going back?

Rowing

Sit down with your legs in front of you.
I'll sit behind, we're part of the crew.

Paddles in the water, row row row.
Row in time and the faster we'll go.

Gymnastics

Arms out, get your balance, feet in line,
Just look at one point and you'll be fine.
Keep your arms out when you walk the beam.

You're an important part of the team.

Go Team

1 2 3

Rugby

Bend over, put one hand on the ground.
You're in a scrum, team mates all around.

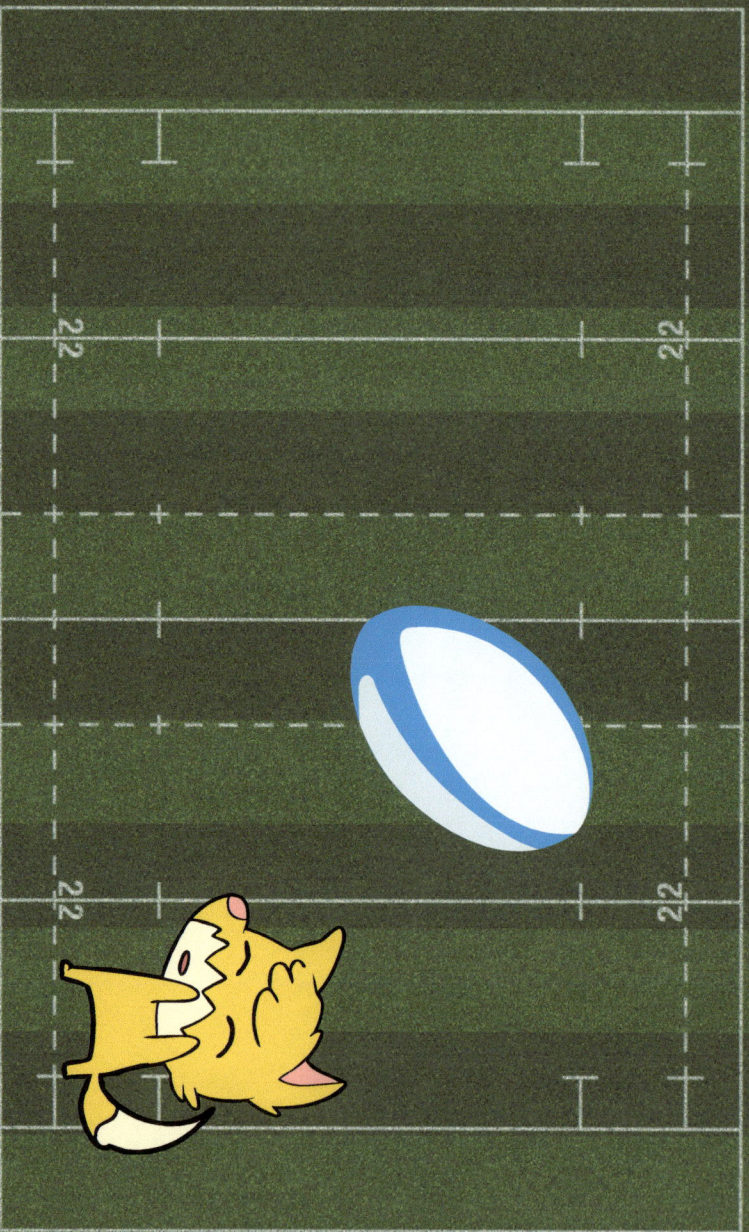

Shall we get ready for a line out?
Throw the ball towards me when I shout.

I caught it! That means we make the call.
Now run as fast as you can with the ball.

Surfing

Jump on your board, put your arms out wide.
Waves are coming, get ready to ride.

You're on a wave, keep your knees bent low.
Like a chilled surfer, go with the flow.

Yoga

Time to relax so breathe in deeply.
If you stay still you may feel sleepy.

Lie down, stretch your arms over your head.
Do this every day just before bed.

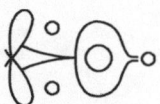

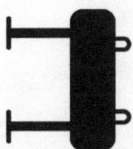

We all know exercise is great to do,
It's the most fun when I do it with you.

www.annastylesauthor.com

Thank you for buying this book,
I hope you enjoyed it.

Also by Anna Styles:

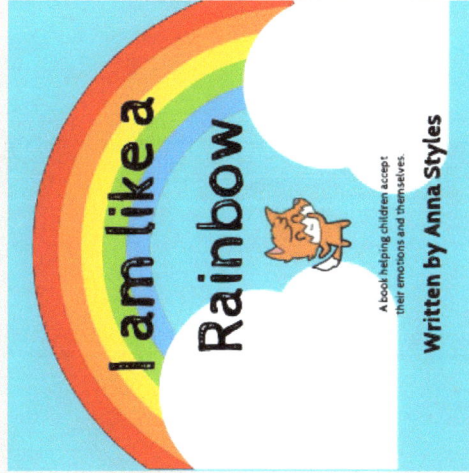

I am like a
Rainbow

A book helping children accept
their emotions and themselves.

Written by Anna Styles

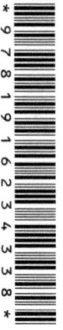